T0132318

A *Rendezvous* with DESTINY

ANISAH HASSAN

Copyright © 2012 by Anisah Hassan. 594740

All rights reserved. No part of this book may be reproduced
or transmitted in any form or by any means, electronic or
mechanical, including photocopying, recording, or by any
information storage and retrieval system, without permission
in writing from the copyright owner.

This is a work of fiction. Names, characters, places and
incidents either are the product of the author's imagination
or are used fictitiously, and any resemblance to any actual
persons, living or dead, events, or locales is entirely
coincidental.

To order additional copies of this book, contact:
Xlibris
844-714-8691
www.Xlibris.com
Orders@Xlibris.com

ISBN: Softcover   978-1-4771-4380-3
        EBook   978-1-4691-2853-5

Print information available on the last page

Rev. date: 05/26/2022

MY MOTHER
GERALDINE SIMPSON

YOUR THE BEAT TO MY HEART
THE MELODY TO MY SONGS
YOU'RE LOVED BY ALL
WHEN I'M WITH YOU NOTHING CAN GO WRONG

MY FATHER
ADOLF
"SWEET POTATO"
ELLISON

I THINK OF YOU ALL THE TIME
YOU WERE MY TALKING BUDDY
ONE OF A KIND

In the name of God, The Beneficent, The Merciful

Geraldine Simpson: My mother, one of the strongest, smartest woman I know. Don't forget to remember how much I love you.

Bridget Simpson: My twin sister, keep the laughter coming. Thanks for doing for my mom what I am unable too. Remember I'm always with you when you're right.

Nathaniel Dear: My brother from another mother (Margie Lee). I want to thank you for telling me like it is even when I don't want to hear it. You're the yin to my yang.

Aletrice (Akua) Walker: My sister with wisdom beyond. The voice of reason, vision of beauty, my zen. I know I'm a challenge, but continue to hang in there with me.

Louise "Weezy" Johnson and Gloria Green: My precious Godmothers. Thanks for caring and trying to teach me lessons to live by

Angela, Darryl, Robin, Dennis Eric Simpson: You are my mother's pride and joy. You make her happy, therefore, whats mine is yours. Love you.

Melissa, Danielle, Kandies, Kiana, Erica, Brittany, Rachelle, Shonte, Sierra, Keisha, Kelly, Gabriellyah, Terrell, Tia: You are all diamonds in the rough. Here's to use growing closer. I hope I've been a positive influence on you. Continue to grow and blossom for I am watching and learning dear ones.

Bro Sultan Muhammad: As Salaam Alaikum to you and your family, hang in there my beloved brother.

Dr. Muhammad Al-Lozi: As Salaam Alaikum to you. Thanks for the wisdom and knowledge you share and making sure I get the very best care.

Dr. Tipu Sultan: As Salaam Alaikum to you. Thanks for all the wisdom and knowledge. Continue to try to teach your sister, and providing the best of care.

Dr. Deloris Greebe- Jones: Thanks for all the knowledge and things you are teaching me every week. I'm stronger you know!

Marty, Tina, Nina: Your'e the best. Keep up the good work. Thanks for bearing with me and knowing my needs for Doc.

BJC Floor of Neurology: To all the nurses, techs, housekeepers for all hugs and kisses every month. Dietary you make me happy, I thank you for accommodating my diet. You all make things easier for me and I love you for that.

Mrs. Purnell: Elementary School Teacher. You encouraged me to write and made me stand before the many laughing school children to read and recite poetry for my grade. I'm better because of that!

Mrs. Scott: My Enrichment lab teacher that taught me poetry and allowing me to choose my own reports to write. Remember Mrs. Scott? My first report was Phyllis Wheatley.

Special thanks to the many Holistic and Naturalpathic MD's and Practitioners that have treated and guided me along the way.

Too all of those unnamed, but have extended kindness to me, I bestow my deepest thanks I am deeply appreciative off all my friends, family, and acquaintances, who merit special mention and have my love.

Author/Poet Foreword
"LIFE'S PERSPECTIVE: LIVING OR SIMPLY EXISTING"

Are you living a life of happiness, success, and peace, or are you simply existing? To live the afore mentioned is something rich and rare indeed. The truth is, a seed must be planted to bring forth enhancing and fulfilling experiences. I would like to think that happiness is waiting somewhere. I'm speaking of true happiness with love all around, filling the atmosphere and consuming the very core of the soul. We all have different interpretations of defining such a state of being.

I'll tell you a little about me. My name is Anisah Hassan. I suffer from a very rare neurological disease, with many auto-immune disorders called Moersch-Woltman/Stiff Person Syndrome, but it doesn't define me. I often lose all control of my body with it's betrayal and intrusive pain, ridgity, and distressing full body spasms. Time and time again destiny and fate decide to take over under the directives of the Almighty One saying "Anisah, you are granted the right to pick yourself up, dust off and start over again". I'm thankful for my blessings of maintaining the ability to access, analyze and make rational decisions. At times, I think to myself, what would you do with a mind, body, and spirit operating harmoniously, all at the same time? Ahh, what a beautiful feeling, full of sweet reveries. With maintaining a sharp mind, I still believe with proper treatment where eastern and western methods of treatment meet, all thing are possible. No confinements or restrictions. What a feeling. It fills my heart, and I smile inside with just the mere thought. Imagine summer days and dancing in the rain. I won't waste a single moment. You're welcomed to join me in this space and time. I'm going to stay awhile. I'm a firm believer, that although things may not be easy I will stick by my course of plans and aspirations. It warms my heart knowing that things can possibly get easier. With this impediment of Stiff Person Syndrome, I must consistently seek wisdom and find the strength to adjust by making crucial life decisions. With all of Stiff Person Syndrome's rude intuitions, my life seems so uncertain at times, yet with a personal relationship with my God, the all knowing, the loving I am equipped to handle life's challenges, and possess the spiritual insight to endure. I can face all adversarial forces with a degree of strength, courage and wisdom.

I'm a music connoisseur, author, and poet. These are some things to help me though the day. I'm remembering my 7th grade teacher Mrs Purnell, and my enrichment lab teacher Mrs. Scott. For our grade we had to stand before the class and resight our assigned poetry for the week. Me, the reserved, and shy child, didn't mind memorizing the poems, nor writing my own. When it came down to getting in front of the class, that's where the problems began. I would speed thought it, only to be told to get back up there if I wanted an A. Reluctantly I did so, with lots of laughs and giggles from my peers. I thank them all, the teachers for enriching my life, and the children for thinking things were funny. It has made me who I am today.

I saw Mrs Scott from, Ford Middle School, In the grocery store,as an adult a couple of years ago. I stood at attention and resighted the poem "Dreams" by Langston Hughes. Flawless I tell you, only thing was I said by Robert Frost (honest mistake). She took me by the arm turned me around and popped me on my bottom as she corrected me "That's Langston Hughes", Now give me a hug, as tears streamed from her eyes."I still remember the "The Voice of a Poet", I replied proudly, "Yes I do." I felt so good and she was so very proud of me. I thanked her for all that she taught me.

So here we are. I ask you and myself, are we living a life of happiness, success, and peace full of enriching experiences or are we simply existing?

Enjoy these words straight from my heart.

Peace and Blessings

Anisah

LET'S BUILD A NATION

LET'S BUILD A NATION WHERE THERE'S NO FRUSTRATION.

NO COMPLICATIONS.
NO CONFRONTATION.
NO EXPLOITATION.

OUR NATION WILL CONSIST OF PURIFICATION.

FRESH VEGETATION.
NICE RELAXATION.
HIGH EXPECTATIONS.

WHY ABIDE WITH A NATION OF MISINTERPRETATION.

POOR REPRESENTATION.
SUCH MISAPPROPRIATION.
THE CURRENT MENTAL RESERVATIONS.

LET'S BUILD A NATION I SAY.
LET'S BUILD A NATION.

OUR NATION WILL BE BUILT UPON REVITALIZATION.

JOY AND ELATION.
MUCH CELEBRATION.
MIND ENRICHMENT.
AND SELF DETERMINATION.

LETS BUILD A NATION.

A RENDEZVOUS WITH DESTINY

I'm on a rendezvous with destiny
Destination, greatness an undeniable necessity
Despite adversity trying to get the best of me
Cast it aside, it's ordained, that it will be

I'm on a rendezvous with destiny
I feel the atmosphere all around simply beaming
Oh no this is not simply me and my daydreaming
It's high beyond the stars, way far exceeding

I'm on a rendezvous with destiny
I'm good, feels great, and I'm so free
Weeding out all foolishness of every degree
It's on, full force, set forth just for me

And on this rendezvous with destiny
That won't, can't and will not stop
Infinity, eternity superseding all naysayers,
I'm on top
Did you hear me, want the entire world to know, I'm on top

Can you feel me? Do you see me? Unbelievable won't you agree?
Inconceivable, beyond thoughts,
what's going to be will be
This fate decreed and ordained, just for thee
This is real, it's reality and it's all for me

I love it, it's on, I truly feel that I can fly
Feels like I'm gliding,
I'm floating look out I've taken to the sky.
This rendezvous with destiny,
truly I'm fortunate I can't deny.
Peace and blessing to all, as I smile, I owe all praises due to The Most High!

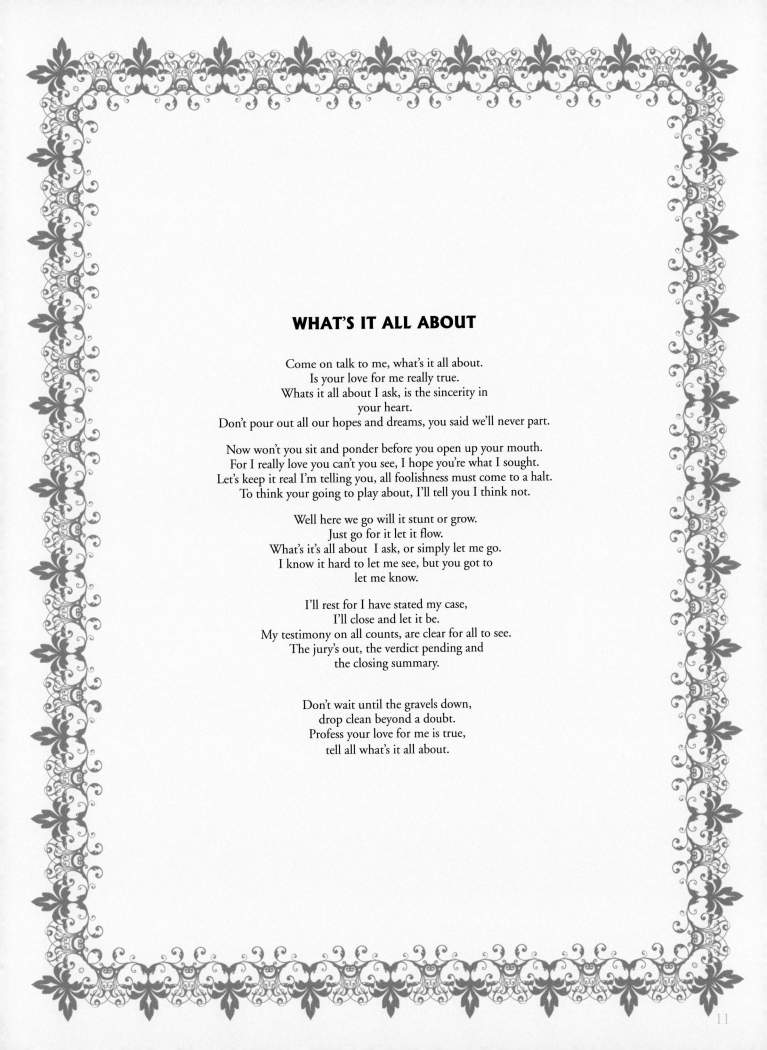

WHAT'S IT ALL ABOUT

Come on talk to me, what's it all about.
Is your love for me really true.
Whats it all about I ask, is the sincerity in
your heart.
Don't pour out all our hopes and dreams, you said we'll never part.

Now won't you sit and ponder before you open up your mouth.
For I really love you can't you see, I hope you're what I sought.
Let's keep it real I'm telling you, all foolishness must come to a halt.
To think your going to play about, I'll tell you I think not.

Well here we go will it stunt or grow.
Just go for it let it flow.
What's it's all about I ask, or simply let me go.
I know it hard to let me see, but you got to
let me know.

I'll rest for I have stated my case,
I'll close and let it be.
My testimony on all counts, are clear for all to see.
The jury's out, the verdict pending and
the closing summary.

Don't wait until the gravels down,
drop clean beyond a doubt.
Profess your love for me is true,
tell all what's it all about.

DEPTHS OF MY SOUL

FROM THE DEPTHS OF MY SOUL
EVEN WHEN I GROW OLD
YOU'LL ALWAYS HAVE MY HEART

YOU WERE MEANT FOR ME
I KNOW THIS TO BE INDEED
I'LL TELL YOU WERE I'LL START

FIRST OUR HEARTS OR INTERTWIND
NOW THAT'S AN EXCELLENT SIGN
TRUE HEARTS TOGETHER AS ONE IS SUCH A INCREDIBLE, UNBREAKABLE BIND

WOW THAT'S JUST ONE OF A KIND
AT LEAST IN SOMES LIFETIME
STOP, LISTEN, LET YOU'RE MIND RUN FREE
LET'S SEE WHAT YOU WILL FIND

AND WHATS THIS AT THE DEPTHS OF MY HEART
PURE WARMTH IT'S NEVER COLD
I MUST SUBSTAIN RIGHT FROM START

THIS LOVE OF OURS WILL NEVER END
YOU ARE MY LOVER AND FRIEND

DON'T LET THE SUN GO DOWN ON ME

DON'T LET THE SUN GO DOWN ON ME.

I LOVE IT, LOVE IT, LOVE IT ON EVERY DEGREE.

KISSED MY FACE, CHEEK, AND HAIR SO GENTLY.

IT MAKES ME FEEL GOOD DELIGHTFUL AND OH SO FREE.

COME LONG MY HONEY I'M SURE YOU'LL AGREE.

WE'LL WIGGLE OR TOE'S LAY OUT BY THE SEA.

WE'LL LAUGH AND PLAY LETTING OR FEELINGS RUN FREE.

OH PLEASE DON'T LET THE SUN GO DOWN ON ME.

DRIVEN

Driven to be the very best
Driven to live with much love and zest
Driven to give with an "S" on my chest
Driven packing peace, the earth I'll infest

Driven to be all that I can
Driven to show the whole world just exactly who I am
Driven to drop pearls of wisdom from Japan to Sudan
Driven to lead the masses with the master plan

Driven to shine all the days of my life
Drive to dispel all ignorance and strife
Driven to step up and fight for what's right
Driven can't help it, must follow the light

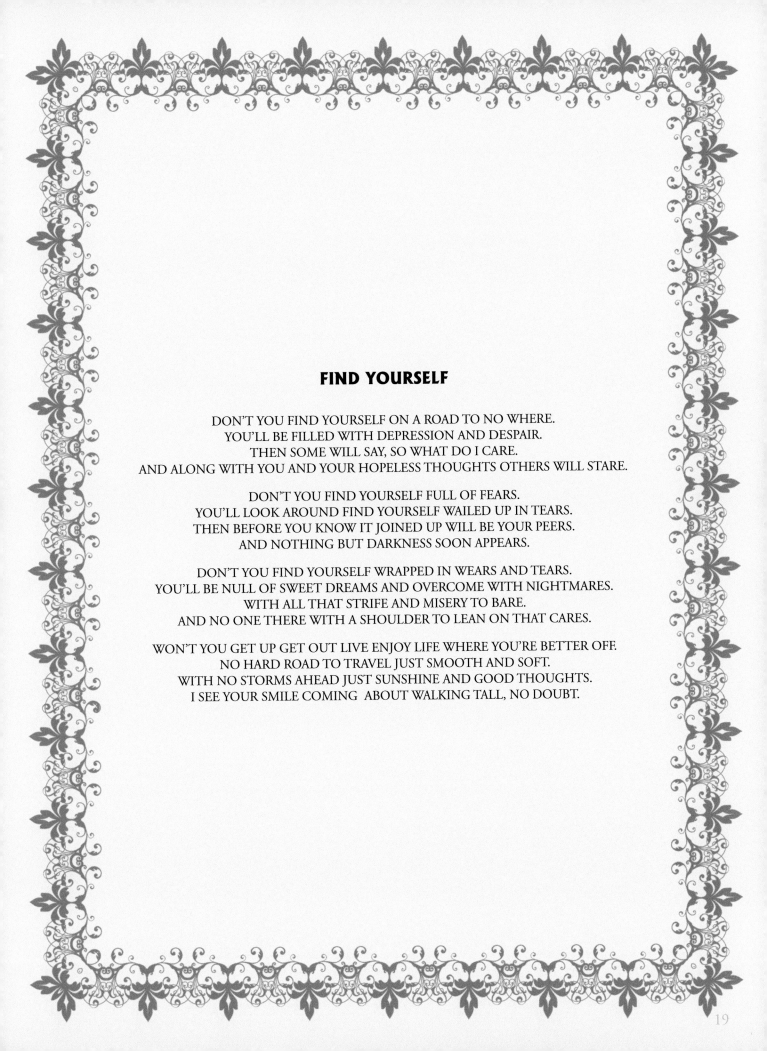

FIND YOURSELF

DON'T YOU FIND YOURSELF ON A ROAD TO NO WHERE.
YOU'LL BE FILLED WITH DEPRESSION AND DESPAIR.
THEN SOME WILL SAY, SO WHAT DO I CARE.
AND ALONG WITH YOU AND YOUR HOPELESS THOUGHTS OTHERS WILL STARE.

DON'T YOU FIND YOURSELF FULL OF FEARS.
YOU'LL LOOK AROUND FIND YOURSELF WAILED UP IN TEARS.
THEN BEFORE YOU KNOW IT JOINED UP WILL BE YOUR PEERS.
AND NOTHING BUT DARKNESS SOON APPEARS.

DON'T YOU FIND YOURSELF WRAPPED IN WEARS AND TEARS.
YOU'LL BE NULL OF SWEET DREAMS AND OVERCOME WITH NIGHTMARES.
WITH ALL THAT STRIFE AND MISERY TO BARE.
AND NO ONE THERE WITH A SHOULDER TO LEAN ON THAT CARES.

WON'T YOU GET UP GET OUT LIVE ENJOY LIFE WHERE YOU'RE BETTER OFF.
NO HARD ROAD TO TRAVEL JUST SMOOTH AND SOFT.
WITH NO STORMS AHEAD JUST SUNSHINE AND GOOD THOUGHTS.
I SEE YOUR SMILE COMING ABOUT WALKING TALL, NO DOUBT.

HOLD ME TIGHT

NOW HOLD ME TIGHT ALL THROUGH THE NIGHT.
I GUARANTEE ASSURED MUCH DELIGHT.
A FIRE I SAY I'M SURE WE'LL IGNITE.
COME CLOSE TO MY SWEET LOVE, I'LL GIVE YOU THE RIGHT.
GET READY GET SET FOR A MOON LIT NIGHT.
THEN HOLD ME TIGHT WITH ALL YOUR MIGHT.

THERE'S SOMETHING IN YOUR EYES I SEE.
THAT GLARE THAT GLOW IS IT JUST FOR ME.
WHILE LETTING OUR FEELINGS RUN WILD AND FREE
YOU KNOW TO MY HEART YOU HOLD THE KEY.
THEN WE'LL BATHE IN DELIGHT.
COME HOLD ME TIGHT, HOW BEAUTIFUL IT WILL BE.

I HOPE YOU DON'T MIND

It's been so long since I've heard the sound of bluebirds singing to me.
That's because I've allowed my spirit to decline so low, I couldn't hear or see.
That was then, and this is now, I'm new in many ways.
No compromise to what the adversary may say.
It's time for change, I determine my destiny, seeing growth day by day.
I HOPE YOU DON'T MIND

And I'm guilty of being a chatter box, my defense to hide things that concerns self.
Well silence is gold, let my soul be exposed.
I'm good not concerned with images painted by no one else.
I HOPE YOU DON'T MIND.

Looking back on all the mistakes I've made, I'd say too much lending of self.
To prove to others my worth, my value, too high a cost to be kept.
What nonsense I got lost in, what could I been thinking, what message did I send.
I was born a winner, innate to strong to bend, starting within this madness ends.
I HOPE YOU DON'T MIND.

And what about the pain I've caused, unbeknownst to me, but nevertheless.
I press harder toward the betterment of me, aleving a mess of stress.
Won't walk around depressed, step aside negativity, as my success blossom and progress.
I know who I am, I know what I want, and I will not settle for less.
I HOPE YOU DON'T MIND.

I've been tossed around, turned upside down by the storms of this cruel world.
Allowed this brilliant mind to sink to lows, almost destroyed you just don't know.
But now I stand on solid ground, wicked elements leave me be.
Some just can't stand triumph from drama, and will bring it on every degree.
I HOPE YOU DON'T MIND

It's old, I'm done it doesn't reside here, let go wont you agree?
As far as I'm concerned I only see stars, what's going to be will be.
I'm golden, upward bound and on the move, chasing rainbows across the sea.
Move over step aside, I'm coming through as all my troubles flee.

I LEAVE MY FEARS BEHIND

I LEAVE MY FEARS BEHIND.
BUT DON'T GO IN BLIND.
YOU SHOULD COME WITH AND YOU WILL FIND.
YOU'LL EXCEL WITH A PEACE OF MIND.

CALM, COOL AND REFINED.
REALLY SMOOTH ON MY GRIND.
LIKE A LIONESS I ROAR, I SMILE I SHINE.
WITH THE WORLD AS MY CHILD, IF ONLY IN MY MIND.

I LEAVE MY FEARS BEHIND.
LIKE A GENTLE WIND INTERTWINED.
WITH ALL THINGS GREAT AND ALIGNED.
I FIND I GET BETTER WITH TIME.

SO KEEP MY HEAD STRAIGHT, I'M AMONGST THE SUBLIME.
AND WITH THAT SAID THERES NO MOUNTAIN THAT I CAN'T CLIMB

I'M A STRANGER HERE

I'm a stranger here in this old world.
Must reestablish my intellectual and moral capacity with grace and much tenacity.
No use for hesitation, it's fact you see.
New horizons, brighter stars are waiting for me.

I'm a stranger here in the misdt of friends.
But, it's my soul that cries out relax, let the sunrays radiate in.
Although it feels different, I know it's truth singing out from within.
I'll hold tight, stand still, and watch the manifestation begin.

I'm a stranger here in my home.
Memories of prior scenes, slowly dissipating almost gone.
My heart races, it pounds, as my mind ponders upon what's really going on?
You are changing my love, dancing to an unknown rhythm, a new song.

I'm not afraid, but it's different, that I must admit.
I'm going to ride, come to far, and I will not quit.
It's peculiar I know, that I can't deny.
Deprivation of ignorance, manifestation of righteous assembly, I think I'll give it a try.

Seeking the inhabitance of the indigenous, peep the sites, then see what I will find.
And whom shall I allow to step into the folds of my mind.
Proceed with caution young heart, steady your gait then define.
Change is good, embraced with solace of mind go on my dear be surprised at what you may find.

Alright I'm sure, I'm ready for my prescribed flight.
Quite sure there awaits me, peace love and happiness, what warmth and delight!

IT WOULD BEHOOVE ME

It would behoove me not to state my case.
It would behoove me not to finish the race.
It would behoove me to turn away a warm embrace.
It would behoove me to leave you feelings misplaced.

Yes I'm the one with impeccable style and grace.
Yes I'm that one with the dazzling smile on my face.
Yes I'm the one that's intricate and pretty like lace.
Yes I'm that one with a queen's knowledge base.

It would behoove me to ignore my greatness and not to recognize.
It would behoove me not to halt the world and make all realize.
It would behoove me not to stand on the front line and fight.
It would behoove me not to expand the minds of the world so they do what's right.

JOYS OF LIFE

IT'S THAT SPIRIT OF KINDNESS THAT OFTEN SURPRISE
IT'S THAT BEING THAT FLOWS EASY THAT FREE'S THE MIND.
IT'S THAT EXTENDED HAND THAT SHOWS THE MEASURE OF A MAN.
IT'S THOSE ARMS THAT EMBRACE THAT BRINGS THAT SMILE UPON THE FACE.

SO WEAR THAT KINDNESS THAT OFTEN SURPRISE.
BE DELIGHTED BY ALL THE SPLENDID THINGS THAT YOU MY FIND.
AND THE JOYS OF LIFE THAT FLOWS EASY.
SENDING THE HAPPINESS FROM ONE SOUL.
OPEN YOUR HEART, AND EXPLORE.

SUIT UP MEASURED MAN WITH THE EXTENDED HAND.
THE MOST COMPASSIONATE HAVE A MASTER PLAN.
AND THOSE ARMS THAT'S WARM AND THERE WITH A WARM EMBRACE.
ENJOY YOUR LOVING WELCOME FROM EAST WEST AND EVERY PLACE.

MATTERS OF THE HEART

When it comes to matters of the heart.
Logic of the mind subsides and doesn't count.
Emotional, physical, spiritual scars.
Impairs the dome, dulls the senses, whirling, twirling destination mars.

When it comes to matters of the heart.
Things can be wonderful, well where shall I start.
Like the sun the stars the moon above.
Naw bigger than that, it's that thing called love.

When it comes to matters of the heart.
One either comes alive or all apart.
My soul cries out with glee, other times
there's strain.
Indication of time to purge, step out and let it rain, let it rain.

Matters of the heart are strange you know.
Never can tell, will it nurture the mind, will I grow.
What ever the case don't trip into a whirl wind,
no spins.
Just affirm to the world over and over again.
I'll ride this journey and lean toward the light, I'LL WIN, I'LL WIN!!!

OOOH I JUST LOVE YOU

Let's write beautiful lyrics together and sing them in perfect harmony.
You are so sweet in my review.
I'll watch you as you sleep at night.
And wonder if it's of me dreaming.
Is it possible? Can it be true?
Then could I possibly have your heart.
You're worth my every thought.

And oooh my dear I want you near.
You're wonderful to behold.
These thoughts will not go cold.
You're valued and respected, and cannot be sold
or brought.

Your heavenly visit to me in my dreams
I anticipate times of sleep.
A spirit of fun and love when I awake.
I tell you, now that's deep.

Oooh I just love you, lead the way and I will
gladly follow.
Now that mean morning, noon and night, and all of our tomorrows.
You're all that I'm thinking of I glow.
And true love never dies.
It just grows as time go by.
I adore you from your head to toe.

Oooh I love you so,
You have to know, just what you mean to me.
A love with respect and honor of the very
highest degree.
Oooh I just love you so I hope that you can see.
Because it's really true dear one.
Forever it will be.

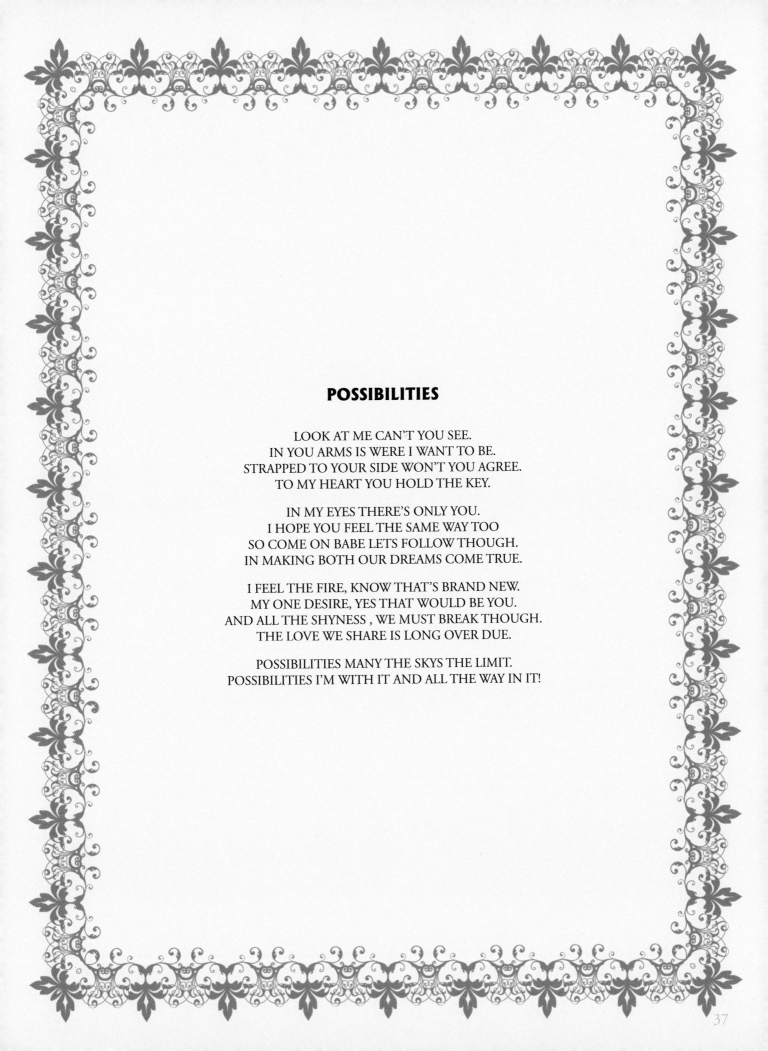

POSSIBILITIES

LOOK AT ME CAN'T YOU SEE.
IN YOU ARMS IS WERE I WANT TO BE.
STRAPPED TO YOUR SIDE WON'T YOU AGREE.
TO MY HEART YOU HOLD THE KEY.

IN MY EYES THERE'S ONLY YOU.
I HOPE YOU FEEL THE SAME WAY TOO
SO COME ON BABE LETS FOLLOW THOUGH.
IN MAKING BOTH OUR DREAMS COME TRUE.

I FEEL THE FIRE, KNOW THAT'S BRAND NEW.
MY ONE DESIRE, YES THAT WOULD BE YOU.
AND ALL THE SHYNESS , WE MUST BREAK THOUGH.
THE LOVE WE SHARE IS LONG OVER DUE.

POSSIBILITIES MANY THE SKYS THE LIMIT.
POSSIBILITIES I'M WITH IT AND ALL THE WAY IN IT!

WHAT'S UP WITH THAT

WHATS' UP WITH THAT? YOU KNOW WHAT I MEAN.
EXPOSED FOR WHAT YOU ARE AND YOU ARE SEEN.
DISGUISED AS MY SISTA,
LIKE YOUR MY BRO.
THAT'S JUST FOR YOUR CONVIENIENCE YOU KNOW THAT I KNOW.

AM I TO BLAME OH NOOOO!

WHAT'S UP WITH THAT? YOU KNOW WHAT I MEAN.
DON'T LOOK ME UP AND DOWN.
THE AL-NOOR IS WHO YOU'LL ANSWER TO WHEN TIME COMES AROUND.
OH NO I'M NOT THE ONE, MERE ONE, JUST TURN WE BETTER DEPART.
YOU NEED MORE THAN I HAVE TO GIVE TO MELT THAT COLD COLD HEART.

AM I TO BLAME NOW DON'T MAKE
ME START.

WHAT'S UP WITH THAT, YOU KNOW WHAT I MEAN.
AT ANOTHERS EXPENSE ALWAYS GOING TO EXTREMES
CREATING ENVY AND STRIFE, BUT WE KNOW WHAT YOU'RE ABOUT.
EXTRA EXTRA EXTRA IN EVERY WAY.
BEYOND THE NORM NO NEED TO FRONT DAY IN DAY OUT.

AM I TO BLAME? SELF INSPECT
YOU'RE CAUGHT.

WHAT'S UP THAT, YOU KNOW
WHAT I MEAN.
SIMPLY REFUSE TO BE YOUR BLAME.
JUST BE YOURSELF, I KNOW YOU'LL BE LOVED JUST THE SAME.
WITHOUT A DOUBT YOU MUST LEAD WITH YOUR HEAD, GUT, AND HEART.
GET THE STRENGHT AND COURAGE TO BE TRUE TO THYSELF.
SHAKE OF THE EGO AND FIND YOURSELF RISING TO THE TOP.

THE PRESENCE OF THE OMINPOTENT

In the eyes of a child.
Reading a book with a smile.
Or hanging out with a friend for awhile.

Strolling the land hand in hand.
Thinking of a master plan.
Or just the change for betterment,
by a single command.

I'm in the Presence of the Omnipotent.

Supreme warmth felt all around
The touch of and extended palm when I'm down.
Or maybe visions encouraging me to reach my higher ground.

Witnessing cleansing rainfall mid abound.
Spring first rainbow when first found.
Jubilant melodies, how sweet the sound.

I'm in the Presence of the Omnipotent.

The Most GRACIOUS THE MOST LOVING, THE LIGHT.
Is all I want to know.
THE PROTECTOR FROM ALL HARM, THE BENEFICENT, THE MERCIFUL.
Is all that's needed to grow.

Unlimited power, miracles performed by the second, minute, hour.
Let it rain on me pour your blessings with showers.
That's what I pray each and everyday.
I long to know you better, need your approval,
in everyway.

I'll shout out you acknowledgment.
There's non greater, I give you all the praise.
It is the profound thought of you, that lives me in a daze.
You've been with me through highs and lows, and through life's every phrase.
Oh Omnipotent, everywhere I am there's the whisper of your name.

SOME MAY SAY

Some may say that, I'm strong consistent, full of hope and I'm anew.
Some say keep your head up you'll pull though, there's always tomorrow, at times I'm sad and blue.
I ask myself.

What do they see?
What do they see?

Some may ask who I am , what planet or mothershp did you come from.
Some wonder where I draw strength and courage, when troubles come.
I ask myself

How do I answer?
How do I answer?

Some may say You may as well give in, go ahead and surrender.
Some say you're though, when the storms of life come, when that tiny ray of light fades to a mere glimmer,
and triumph seems slender.
I ask myself.

But what do they know?
What do they know?

Some may say, ahh that's a no brainer, not worth your precious time.
Some say you're wasting energy, don't let those issues infiltrate your mind.
I must remind them, I'll determine what cause
I'll bear.
It's what I choose, mull and analyze if you care.
I ask myself.

Do they dare?
Do they dare?

Some may say, stop to exhale, you should relax, fall back, fade to black.
Some may say, Oh no you don't, stand strong, hold firm, you don't have the luxury to go lax.
I ask myself.

What do I do?
What do I do?

One things definite, no doubt, for sure,
I KNOW THYSELF.
Do me at all times, yet never forget the importance to share peace and love to everyone else.

Printed in the United States
by Baker & Taylor Publisher Services